HOW TO:
PASS THE
DMV
COMMERCIAL
PRE-TRIP
INSPECTION
STUDY-GUIDE
BY BRIAN A GARCIA

Study Guide

I want to express my gratitude for joining me on this journey towards obtaining a class A or B license/permit. The focus of this book is on the essential skills required for the DMV walk-through, including in-cab and air brakes inspections. All are necessary for obtaining a CDL permit in California. The objective is not only to gain knowledge but also to comprehend the truck as a driver. Having been a driver in the past and now working as a technician in the industry, my aim is to assist others in achieving this goal. Passing the DMV test can appear challenging; this is why this book covers the steps required to succeed. The booklet is a source of knowledge that is simple and straight to the point. Once you complete it, there should be no difficulty in obtaining the permit or passing the skill test for your license. Let's begin!

Brian A Garcia
Los Angeles,California

LIST OF COMPONENTS

Truck Outside Inspection:

- Marker lights
- Windshield Wipers
- Windshield
- Hood
- Grill
- Headlight Housing
- Convex Mirrors
- Bumper
- Fog Lights
- License Plate
- Engine Air-Filter
- Air Filter Gauge Reminder
- All Hoses
- All Clamps
- Exhaust Gas Recirculation
- Turbo
- Alternator
- A/C-Compressor
- Starter
- Tensioner/ Pulley
- All Belts
- Fan Blades
- Shrouds
- Radiator
- Condenser
- Air Dryer
- Filters
- Starter
- Frame

- Leaf Springs/Leaf Spring Mounts
- Oil Filler
- Shock Absorbers
- Axles
- Tie Rod Arm
- Brake Hose
- Brakes-Chamber
- Slack-Adjuster
- S-Cam
- Brake Shoes
- Brake Drums
- Tires
- Rims
- Axle Hub Cap
- Lug Nuts
- Dip Stick
- Coolant Tank
- Mounting Brackets
- Power Steering Reservoir
- Water Separator
- Water Pump
- Steering Shaft
- U-joints
- Gear Box
- Pit-man Arm
- Draglink
- Steering Arm
- Kingpins
- Foot Valve
- Fuse Box
- Power Steering Pump
- Air Compressor

- Driver Side Door
- Weather strips
- The Hand Rail\Grab-Handle
- Mirrors
- Steps
- Batteries
- Air Tanks
- Dot Stickers
- MarkerLights/Turn Signals
- Catwalk/Deck
- Air Lines
- 7-way Green Cord Connector
- Def Tank
- Drive line
- Fifth Wheel
- Drive Axles
- Differentials
- Pintle Hook
- MudFlaps/Hangers
- Conspicuity Tape
- Registration/Trailer
- Cross Members
- Landing Gear/ Crank Handle
- Torsion Bar
- Air Bags
- Trailer Rug Guard
- Hinges
- Exhaust
- Heat Shield
- Exhaust Supporting Rod

1.
PHRASES TO REPEAT

■ During the examination, ensure that all components are not bent, cracked or broken, and are not cut, ripped, orn or frayed. Check for any signs of damage or leaks on he vehicle, and ensure that there are no exposed wires, llegal tape or cut wires on the electrical components. Also, verify that there are no illegal drilled holes on the chassis frame, and that everything is properly mounted, ncluding the bolts. Touch each component and inform the DMV instructor that they are properly mounted and secure to demonstrate your understanding of their ocation. Remember to repeat the highlighted phrases during the walkthrough test.The order in which you conduct the examination is crucial. Begin with the exterior walkthrough, followed by the in-cab inspection, and finally, complete the air brakes test. This approach eliminates the need to repeat the exterior and in-cab tests if you fail the air brakes test. With this book in your hands, the kelihood of failing is minimal.

ORDER OF WALK THROUGH INSPECTION

To commence the walk-through, start by ensuring the vehicle is safely parked. Apply the wheel chocks securely prior to beginning the external examination. Taking precautions and adhering to safety measures is paramount at the DMV, making this step all the more essential. You'll then proceed to the front of the truck ready to begin the examination, speaking loudly and clearly to communicate each step to the DMV representative. The first step will take place in the front of the tractor and may involve some intentional repetition to ensure it is dine thoroughly. This is a 10 step walkthrough.

Step 1

The Front Inspection: Start from the top of the truck and make your way to the bottom.

Marker Lights- The five amber marker lights are securely mounted and in proper working condition. There are no visible signs of damage, cracks, or bending. The three center lights signify that this vehicle is commercial, and all lights on the vehicle are functioning correctly.

The Windshield:Windshield Wipers-The windshield and wipers are in good condition and free from any visible damage, such as bending, cracking, or breakage. No illegal stickers are present on the windshield, ensuring an unobstructed view. The wipers are working correctly, and their functionality can be tested during an in-cab inspection. All components, including the wipers and windshield washer tank, are securely mounted and properly secured.

The Hood,Headlight Housing, and Grill- All the components are securely mounted and properly secured. The hood is free from any visible damage, such as bending, cracking, or breakage, and the hood latches are securely mounted to the truck to prevent the hood from flying open while driving. The headlights are in proper working order and can be demonstrated, including the high beams, low beams, turn signals, and emergency lights. The grill is also securely mounted and free from any signs of damage, such as bending, cracking, or breakage.

Hood/Convex Mirrors- The hood mirrors are securely mounted, and all bolts are properly connected, ensuring no visible damage to the housing or mirrors. Additionally, all items on the hood itself are intact.None of the items are bent cracked or broken.

Bumper- The bumper is securely mounted and properly fastened, free from any visible damage, such as bending, cracking, or breakage. The license plate is also securely mounted, displaying all legible numbers and letters.

Next, during the inspection, you will check the underside of the vehicle and report the following to the instructor: There are no visible signs of leaks on the ground, and there are no low hanging components or objects underneath the vehicle.The wires and front axles appear to be securely fastened, with no visible signs of

damage, such as bending, cracking, or breakage. In the first step of the inspection, you will also need to verify that the top of the truck shows no signs of obstruction, then inform the nstructor to follow you to the passenger side. Once there, you will confirm that there are no wires or other objects obstructing your path, and repeat the same on the driver side. In conclusion, there are no visible obstructions preventing the truck and trailer from moving, allowing it to pull out safely.

Step 2

As part of step two, you will proceed to the passenger side of the engine compartment. Before doing so, inform the DMV examiner that you will be opening the hood to continue the walkthrough. To open the hood, place both hands on it and use one foot on the open section of the front bumper for leverage. Once the hood is fully opened, return to the passenger side of the engine compartment, starting from the top and working your way down to the tires. During this process, you will identify the components that are essential for this examination.

Engine Compartment-Starting from the top, you will inspect the engine air filter and air filter gauge, which are connected together. Ensure that the filter gauge is not showing any red or filled readings. Additionally, verify that the filter and its housing are free from any visible damage, such as bending,  cracking, or breakage, and that all bolts are securely mounted. You can refer to the image below for reference.

It is also important to mention the engine air filter's maintenance history during the inspection. Next, inspect the hose and clamp that connects to the engine air filter and confirm that this component is not damaged or broken.

Hoses-Confirm that all hoses connected to components are securely mounted. Notify the DMV examiner that all hoses on the right side of the engine are in good condition, free from any cuts, tears, frays or visible damage. Additionally, there should be no signs of leaks, whether it is air or liquid. To demonstrate this, touch every hose and clamp while informing the examiner that you are ensuring that all the hoses and clamps are securely mounted.

For the A/C line, assure the examiner that there are no freon leaks, which can sometimes be identified by a green substance on a cracked or torn hose.

Refer to image 3, which depicts a Detroit engine, to verify that all components are visible and the hoses are securely mounted.

The EGR (Exhaust Gas Recirculation)- Ensure that the EGR (Exhaust Gas Recirculation) component is securely mounted with all bolts connected properly, and there are no signs of bending, cracking or breaking. Indicate the location of the EGR component by pointing to it, and reference the image provided. Confirm that the clamps are not bent, cracked or broken, and there are no signs of broken welds. Additionally, ensure there are no signs of leaks coming from the EGR.

The Turbo- Verify that the Turbo component is securely mounted and there are no signs of damage such as bending, cracking, or breaking. Check that all bolts on the shield are present and secure. Confirm that the system is functioning properly.

The A/C Compressor- The compressor is firmly mounted and secured, without any damages or looseness. The belt is properly connected to the compressor. The A/C system is operational and can be tested during the in-cab inspection. The A/C lines connected

to the compressor are appropriately fastened and secure, with no indications of leaks. The receiver dryer is also properly mounted and secured to the A/C lines.

The Alternator- The location of the alternator on this engine is below the A/C compressor. The AMPS information is displayed on a small metal plate. Verify that the alternator is securely mounted and there are no signs of damage such as bending, cracking, or breaking. The belt that connects to the alternator should also be securely fastened and not cut, ripped, or torn. Ensure that there are no signs of any illegal tape and no exposed electrical wires.

Starter-The starter can be located on either the left or right side of the frame rail, depending on the vehicle. For a Cummins engine, it is located near the engine block on the right side. Although it may be difficult to find, it is crucial to mention because it is a major component of a truck, and without it, the vehicle would not function. Referencing the image of an Isuzu starter provided, verify that the starter is not bent, cracked, or broken, and that there are no exposed wires.

The Tensioner Pulley-To ensure the security of this component, check for a single bolt that holds it in place. You can verify its stability by slightly pulling on the belt in the front of the engine - it should be taut. It's optional to mention this component during the inspection. If you do mention it, make sure to state that the pulley is not bent, cracked, or damaged.

All Belts/Serpentine- All belts are properly secured and show no signs of being cut, ripped, or torn. The ribs on the belts are in good condition and functioning properly. Belts should have 1/2 to 3/4 inch of play in the center.

The Fan Blades/Shrouds- Ensure that the shroud covering the fan blades is mounted securely. Check for any cracks and ensure that all the clips are secure. Verify that the fan blades are properly mounted and without any broken blades. The fan is operating effectively and all bolts are present.

The Radiator-The radiator is securely mounted and there are no indications of coolant leakage. The fins on the radiator are intact and undamaged, and the radiator itself is not bent, cracked, or broken. All hoses are correctly connected, and the coolant level in the surge tank is adequate.

The Condenser- The condenser is positioned at the front of the radiator and is a critical component of the A/C system. It is securely mounted in place and there are no signs of any damage to its fins. It is important to note that the condenser is not bent, cracked or broken.

The Air Dryer- The air dryer is typically located at the bottom right near the bumper. It's crucial to verify that the air dryer is properly mounted and secure with all bolts connected. Additionally, the clamps and hoses should be secure to the air dryer with no signs of air leaks. During operation, the air dryer should purge when the air brake system reaches the cut-out on the dash gauges. It's important to note that the air dryer should not be bent, cracked, or broken.

The Frame- During the inspection, it's important to also check the frame by pointing at it. The frame should be free from any signs of being bent, cracked, or broken. Additionally, there should be no evidence of any unauthorized welds or drilled holes on the frame rail. All bolts should be properly mounted and secure.

The Leaf Springs and Leaf Spring Mounts- Ensure that the leaf springs are properly mounted and securely attached.

Verify that all spacers are present and that the u-bolts are correctly mounted and secure. Confirm that these components are not bent, cracked, or broken and that there are no signs of any unauthorized welds. Check that the leaf springs have not shifted and that there is no more than a 1/4 inch of missing leaf. Any more than this would result in the vehicle being out of service.

The Shock Absorbers-
Please inspect the shocks on all four corners of the vehicle to ensure they are not leaking and are not bent or broken. Additionally, check the suspension on all corners of the vehicle. No signs of leaks or damage on the shocks.

The Brake Hose- Verify that the brake hose is properly connected to the ABS modulator valve and the brake chamber, with no audible sound for air leaks. Demonstrate to the examiner that the hose is not cut, ripped, or frayed in any way.

The Brake Chamber- When inspecting the brake chamber, ensure that there are no visible signs of leaks from the chamber. Verify that the push rod is properly connected to the slack adjuster and is not cracked. You can refer to the images at the end of the inspection for identifying these components. Additionally, confirm that the brake chamber is not bent, cracked, or broken. Check that the chamber is not leaking and that the stroke does not exceed 2 inches when the brake is pressed.

The Slack Adjusters- When examining the slack adjusters connected to the brake chambers, ensure they are not bent, cracked, or broken, and that the cotter pins and rings are in place. The slack adjusters are connected to the S-cam, which in turn connects to the brake shoes. Proper adjustment of the slack adjusters is important to prevent overheating of the brake shoes and drum. For automatic slack adjusters, use the appropriate tool to tighten the slack adjuster all the way until the brake shoes sit on the drum, and then back it off a quarter turn. Manual slack adjusters on trailers can usually be adjusted with a 9/16 socket and ratchet, but this may vary depending on the truck and trailer system. Remember to set the slack adjuster properly to ensure safe and efficient braking.

S-CAM-In this inspection, it's not possible to see the S-cam as it's located inside where the brake

shoes are. The S-cam is responsible for moving the brake shoes and connecting them with the drums to stop the vehicle. It's important to verify that the S-cam is not bent, cracked, or broken even though it's not visible from the outside. Remember that it's located inside where the brake shoes sit.

The Brake Shoes- When examining the brake shoes, ensure that they have a thickness of at least 8/32nds. If they are thinner than that, both sides of the brake shoes will need to be replaced. Additionally, inspect the brake shoes for any signs of uneven wear or cracked lining. Moving on to the drum, check that it is not cracked, broken, or warped. Ensure that the drum has no signs of uneven wear or grooves on its surface.

The Drum-When examining the drum, ensure that it is mounted securely and there are no visible signs of warping or cracks that extend across the drum. Additionally, check for any signs of a lip that may indicate the drum is worn. It's important to inspect all areas around the truck, unless instructed otherwise by the examiner. There should be no major heat cracks on the drum and the brake shoes should be sitting correctly on the drum surface.

The Tires- Ensure that the tire is securely mounted on the wheel assembly. The recommended tire pressure for the steer tires should be between 110 and 120 psi, and you should confirm that the tire is not flat. Inspect the tire for any signs of toe wear or uneven wear, and check that there are no nails or other foreign objects lodged in the tread. Read the tire sidewall to confirm that the correct size tire and rim are mounted, as well as the type of tire. Additionally, check that the tread depth is no less than 4/32nds, indicating that the tire does not need to be replaced at this time.

The Rims- Ensure that the rims are mounted securely without any signs of being bent, cracked, or broken. Verify that the lug nuts are properly mounted and torqued to specification.

The Axle Hub and Cap- To ensure the proper maintenance of the axle hub, make sure that the cap is securely in place and that the hub is properly filled with fluid. You can check the fluid level by removing the cap and inspecting the lining on the outside of the

hub. Make sure there are no signs of leakage from the hub. Once this has been verified, you can proceed to the next step of the inspection.

Step 3

Moving on from completing step two on the passenger side of the engine compartment, we now proceed to the other side of the engine compartment. It's important to note that everything mentioned on the passenger side during step two also applies to the driver side, except for a few additional components that will be highlighted. For instance, you may mention the brakes and shocks on the driver side, and the inspector might quickly move on to the next section. However, some inspectors may request that you repeat the information from the shocks to the frame and other components. If this happens, simply go over everything again, as it all matches the opposite side.

Now, for step three of the engine compartment inspection, we will mention some of the general knowledge needed for the inspection. These components are not in-depth, but they are necessary to mention. We will begin by pointing out the oil filler location, where you fill the truck with oil.

Oil Filler-The oil filler location can be identified by a cap that is typically marked with a yellow color, although it can sometimes be a red cap. It's important to note that the cap must be in place and not damaged or cracked. The **dipstick** is usually located nearby, so be sure to check the engine's oil level by verifying the level on the dipstick. Inform the inspector that the oil level is at the "full" sign, as this will demonstrate that you have checked the engine's oil level

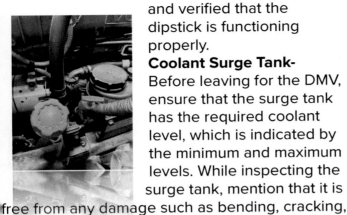

and verified that the dipstick is functioning properly.

Coolant Surge Tank- Before leaving for the DMV, ensure that the surge tank has the required coolant level, which is indicated by the minimum and maximum levels. While inspecting the surge tank, mention that it is

free from any damage such as bending, cracking, or breakage. Additionally, make sure that there are no signs of coolant leaks, and that the hoses connected to the tank are securely mounted. Although not essential, you may also conduct a coolant test using a tester to demonstrate the coolant concentration. Note that the coolant is typically a 50/50 mixture and is not fully concentrated.

Mounting Brackets- It's important to verify that the brackets on both sides of the radiator housing are securely attached and not broken, with the bolts properly mounted and tightened.No signs of rust on the metal.

Power Steering Reservoir-The cream vanilla tank located above the gear box is connected to the gear box, making it easy to identify the hose leading to the power steering reservoir. During inspection, ensure that the tank is mounted securely and there are no signs of leaks from the hoses connected to it. Check the fluid level in the tank and make sure it is at full. Also, verify that the filter inside the tank has been serviced and is not cracked. It's important to note that there is a filter inside the power steering tank. Once you have checked that the filter is in good condition, move on to the next step.

Water Separator/ Oil / Fuel Filters- When inspecting engines, it's important to note that the filter locations may vary depending on the engine model. For instance, on a Detroit engine, the filters are typically located on the left side, whereas on a Cummins engine, the filters are located on separate sides, with the oil filter on the right side. It's crucial to correctly identify the engine to locate the filters and include them in the inspection report. Ensure that all filters are mounted securely and are not damaged, cracked or broken. Check for any signs of oil, fuel or coolant leaks. If the engine has a coolant filter, verify that it is present and in good condition. Once you have confirmed these points, move on to the next step.

All Hoses- As previously mentioned, it's important to check that all hoses and clamps are properly mounted and secure. Additionally, ensure that none of the hoses are cut, ripped, torn, or frayed, and that they are all functioning properly. Double-checking these points will help ensure the safety and reliability of the vehicle.

The Water Pump- Located at the front of the engine face, the water pump is belt-driven and a critical component to inspect. Ensure that it is mounted securely and that there are no signs of coolant leaks. It's important to include this in the inspection report since it is a mandatory item on the checklist. Verify that all bolts holding down the water pump are secure and proceed with the inspection.

The Steering Shaft/ U-Joints- As you inspect the vehicle, ensure that the steering shaft is securely mounted and properly greased. The steering shaft features grease fittings that sit inside the u-joints, so make sure they are all in good condition and not bent, cracked, or broken. Keep in mind that the steering shaft is connected to the gearbox, so it's important to check both components and work your way down as you inspect the vehicle.

Gear Box- Ensure that the gear box is mounted securely and is functioning properly. There should be no signs of damage such as bending, cracking, or breaking. It's also important to note that the gear box is connected to the pitman arm, so be sure to verify that the connection between the two components is properly done and functioning well.

Pitman Arm/ Drag-link/ Steering arm- The pitman arm, drag-link, and steering arm are all interconnected and secured by a castle nut and cotter pins. Ensure that the castle nuts are securely in place with the cotter pins properly installed. Verify

that the pitman arm and drag-link are securely fastened with no excessive play. Also, make sure that the steering arm is properly mounted and securely fastened.

The King-pins- Both sides of the steer axle will have kingpins, with the steering arm on the driver's side connected to the kingpins by the brake shoes. It is important to ensure that the kingpins are adequately lubricated and free of any rust or damage to the metal.

The Foot Valve- Examine the foot valve to ensure that no noticeable leaks can be heard. Additionally, carefully examine all the airline hoses to ensure that there are no small leaks present in the foot valve of the truck.

Fuse Box- The fuse box is typically positioned near the foot valve on the driver's side. Inform the inspector that all fuses are present and not blown. It is worth noting that when you conduct the walk-through, you will need to repeat the same process from the slack adjusters to the exterior of the tires on the opposite side of the vehicle, as each of the components mentioned is located on both sides.

Power Steering Pump- The pump is situated behind the frame, positioned between the engine and the frame. It is important to note the pump's location to the inspector and ensure that it is securely bolted and free of any leaks. Although the pump is not easily visible as it is somewhat concealed, emphasizing its location to the inspector is essential.

The Air Compressor- The air compressor is responsible for generating the air in the system and is connected by a bronze line. The Governor, which can be adjusted to control where the air cuts out, is located on the air compressor. It is important to ensure that the air compressor is securely mounted and free of any air leaks. Confirm that the Governor is also properly mounted and secure, with no signs of damage or wear.

The items that need to be mentioned now are a repeat of step two. These include the Slack Adjuster, brake chamber, brake shoes, drums, leaf springs, u-bolts, spacers for the leaf springs, leaf spring mounts, tires, rims, and lug nuts. As previously mentioned, ensure that each of these components is not bent, cracked, or broken. Upon completing this section, the next step becomes even easier. The following section, step four of the walk-through, will cover the components located on the driver side door side. You can reference the section above for details.

Step 4

The Driver Side Door- To inspect the door, begin by testing the handle to ensure it can be opened and closed with ease. As you open the door, demonstrate to the inspector that the hinges are not damaged and that the door moves smoothly without any issues.

Additionally, verify that the weather strips inside the door are securely in place and are not cut, ripped, or torn.

The HandRail/Grab Handle- Ensure that the grab handle is mounted firmly and securely without any signs of looseness.

xamine the windows on the door to confirm that they are not
roken and can be raised and lowered without any difficulty.

The Mirrors- Verify that the mirrors are securely
mounted to the mirror mount and that there are no
gns of looseness. Check that the mirrors are
roperly adjusted, and make further adjustments
uring the in-cab inspection if necessary. Ensure that
e mirrors are not cracked and are visible for use.

Steps- Check that the steps leading into the cab
re secure and that all bolts are present.
ccasionally, the step may also function as a battery
over. In this case, inform the inspector and
emonstrate how the batteries are situated under
e cover.

Batteries- Inspect the batteries and battery cover, ensuring that
ey are present and there are no signs of corrosion or leaking fluid.

erify that the batteries are securely mounted with a battery hold-
own clamp, and that the cables are clean and connected properly.
heck that the batteries are not damaged in any way.

Air Tanks-Check that the air tanks are labeled as the primary and secondary tanks, and that they are properly mounted and securely fastened with straps. Inform the inspector that the tanks must be drained daily by the end of your driving shift to prevent any water buildup inside. Additionally, inspect the tanks for any signs of damage such as bending, cracking or breaking, and ensure that there are no air leaks in the air lines.

Dot Stickers- It is important to note that the truck must display DOT numbers to verify its information. Please ensure that you mention this during the inspection.

Marker Lights/Turn Signals- Sometimes, the light may be located under the driver side door. Verify that the light is not bent, cracked or broken, and demonstrate its functionality by testing it if requested by the inspector.

Now that Section 4 has been covered, it is time to move on to Section 5 which covers the catwalk sections where the cables and the fifth wheel meet the trailer.

Step 5

Although this section has some smaller details, it is still important for the walk-through examination. The catwalk, also known as the deck plate, must be properly mounted and secured with no bent edges sticking up. Additionally, the plate should not be bent,

racked, or broken and must be safe to walk on for connecting the
irlines.

Air Lines-The service line is represented by the blue air line
ose, while the red airline hose is for the trailer emergency line. Both
nes must be securely connected to the trailer, along with the 7-way
reen cord for the lights. Ensure that the glad hands for the airline
re properly mounted and in good condition, with intact rubber
eals. Check that the hoses are not cracked, pinched, or leaking,
nd that they are not touching the catwalk to prevent any potential
azards. The 7-way cord must be properly connected to the trailer
sing a pin box.

Grab Handle / Steps / Fuel Tanks-The handle that allows you to
valk up and down the catwalk must be securely mounted. The steps
n the catwalk must also be securely attached and free of any sharp

edges or damage. The fuel tanks
must be properly secured using
fuel tank straps, which should have
rubber between the metal strap and
the tank to prevent metal-to-metal
friction. All bolts must be securely
mounted and not show any signs of
illegal welds. The fuel caps will be
located on the tank and the amount
of gallons the tank can hold will be
indicated under the cap to comply
ith regulations.

Def Tank-The DEF tank should be securely
ounted and free of any leaks. In case of a leak, you
ay observe a white substance that resembles
now. Ensure that the cap is properly secured and
erify that the DEF tank is at least 1/8 full. The DEF
nk is easily identifiable as it is blue and often
beled with "DEF" at the cap.

Driveline /Differential- Make sure to check that
e driveline is securely connected and that all the u-
ints are in place. Confirm that the yoke is properly attached to the
ifferential, and that the drive axles are secure. Additionally, check
or any signs of leaks on the differential.

The Fifth Wheel-The fifth wheel plate's pins must be secure and the teeth on the plate must lock the trailer pin in place. The fifth wheel plate can be adjusted as needed and is properly greased for smooth trailer movement. The release handle for the fifth wheel plate must operate properly to release the trailer. None of the mentioned items are bent, cracked, or broken, and there should be no signs of illegal welds. Additionally, the release arm must not be bent or broken.

Below is the image of the fifth wheel and in good condition.

The First Drive Axle and Second Drive Axle-Both of these axles are identical, so it's important to mention to the inspector that everything is the same from this point on the tractor. The inspection process for this axle is similar to that of the steer axle.Ensure that the differential is not leaking and has a secure breather. The s-cam bracket should be mounted and secure with no signs of broken welds. The leaf springs and their mounts should be secure, and the springs should not be cracked. The u-bolts that hold the springs

down should be secure as well.The slack adjusters should be secure, and the pins should be present. They should be working properly, measuring what they need to measure with no more than 1/8th of a difference on both sides. The brake chambers should be mounted and secure, with no audible sounds of leaks. The brake shoes should be mounted and secure with no cracks or missing springs. The brake shoes should measure more than 8/32nds. The drums should be properly mounted and secure with no major cracks or lips that indicate the need for replacement.Moving on to the tires, nsure that they are not cut in any area and that the air pressure is t the proper level. You can find the tire size on the front face of the re alongside the rim size. Ensure that the rim is not damaged or racked and that all lug nuts are secure and torqued to spec. This rocess should be repeated three more times as both axles are lentical.On the back side of the tractor, mention the following three arts.

The Pintle Hook- To ensure safe peration, it's important to inspect the intle hook on the tractor or trailer. Look or any broken welds, and ensure that it's ot bent, cracked, or rusted. If the pintle ook has glad-hands, check for signs of aks and make sure that the rubber seals re intact without any cuts, tears, or frays.

The Mud-flaps-The mud-flaps on both des of the rear end of the truck are secure and have reflectors. he hangers for the mud-flaps are present and not damaged. None f the items mentioned are bent, cracked, or broken. The rear lights, cluding the reverse light and the back-up sound, are functioning roperly. You can demonstrate their operation if requested by the spector. After completing this section, we can move on to step six f the inspection.

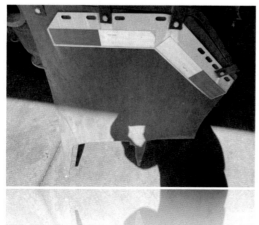

Step 6

this step, you will transition from examining the tractor to specting the trailer components. The trailer should have clean 7-

way connector pins free from any debris. The registration holder should be visibly present on the front of the trailer with the registration up-to-date inside. Ensure the glad hands for the air lines are securely mounted and have new rubber seals.

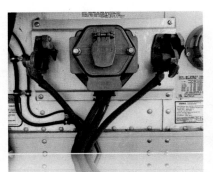  

Cross members-Ensure that all cross members on the trailer are securely in place. It is important to note that there should be no visible holes on the underside of the trailer and no signs of any illegal welds.

Landing Gear- To ensure proper functionality, check the landing

gear handle for any damage such as bending, cracking, or breaking. Make sure that the landing gear goes up and down smoothly and demonstrate this if requested. Additionally, confirm that the landing gear is properly lubricated and all bolts are mounted securely with no signs of loose components.

Lights- It is important to test all the lights on the trailer to ensure they are properly mounted and secure. This includes verifying that the ABS light is functioning properly. Checking the entire lighting ystem at the beginning of the inspection may make the process impler.

Air Line Hoses-Step seven involves hecking the cargo on the trailer. Verify that ne cargo is properly loaded and secured. The ad must not exceed the weight limit and it nust be balanced evenly on both sides. The ad must not be stacked too high or too low nd there should be no signs of shifting uring transit. The cargo must not be azardous or illegal in any way. The cargo nould also be properly labeled and marked ith any necessary warnings or precautions. nce you have verified the cargo, you can ove on to the final step of the inspection.

Step 7

In this step, we will focus on the first axle of the trailer, starting om the inside and moving outwards. Firstly, identify any stickers dicating the tire pressures and any safety warnings present on the ailer. Then, move on to the torsion bar.

Torsion Bar- The torsion bar on both sides mounted securely and there are no signs of ny broken welds. Additionally, the torsion bar not bent, cracked or broken.

Leaf Springs-The leaf springs on both des are securely and properly mounted ithout any cracks, and the u-bolts and nuts olding them in place are present and secure. dditionally, the spacers between them are not amaged or broken.

Brake Chambers/Slack Adjuster- Verify that there are no air aks in the air lines and they are not cut, ripped, or torn. The brake namber should not have any leaks and be properly secured. Check the slack adjuster is set according to the specifications and the ns are present with all components working correctly.

Shocks/Airbags-All of the shocks on both axles of the trailer are operly bolted and mounted without any signs of leaking or amage. This applies to all shocks on the trailer. The airbags are secure and not cut, ripped, or torn, and there are no audible sounds of leakage.

The Brakes and Drums- The brake assemblies are securely in place and have all their springs intact. The brake pads have more than 8/32nds of thickness and are free from cracks or damage. The brake drums are not cracked or excessively worn and are properly secured.

Tires and Rims- The tires are checked for cuts and are inflated to the proper air pressure. The tire treads are checked and must be more than 4/32nds. The rims are inspected for any damage, cracks, or bends. The lug nuts are securely fastened and properly torqued to the studs.

The sliding pin of the trailer is checked for proper function. It should move the trailer back and forth, allowing it to be positioned in a specific location where the holes will align.

Mud-flaps/Hanger- The mud-flaps on both sides are securely in place and not torn. The hanger holding the mud-flaps is free from

ny damage or bending, and all bolts are properly secured to keep
ne mud-flaps in place.Step 8

Trailer Rear

This is going to be the rear section of the trailer where you will
lentify the components on the trailer.

Markers Lights/Taillights/ Signal Lights-All of the lights must be
inctioning properly without any broken, bent, or cracked parts.
dditionally, none of the lights should be inoperative. It may be
ecessary to demonstrate the proper functioning of the lights if
quested by the instructor.

Rug Guard-Ensure there are no broken welds and the
inspicuity tape is visible with no signs of it being bent, cracked, or

oken. Additionally, verify the license plate on the rear and ensure
at the black dock bumpers are present without being damaged or
rn.

Door Hinges/Handles-The hinges and handles on the rear doors of the trailer must be in proper working condition without any signs of breakage. The doors must open and close smoothly without any resistance. As you open the doors, inspect the interior of the trailer for any signs of light peaking through, broken floorboards, or holes in the walls. If the doors do not have hinges, they may have rollers inside, and the hinges may be located internally. This concludes the inspection of the rear trailer section.

Step 9

This step is a repetition of step 7, but on the opposite side of the trailer. The same components need to be inspected, including the **brake chamber, slack adjuster, air bags, axle, air tank, cross members, airline lines, leaf springs, leaf spring mounts and u-bolts, brake shoes, drums, slack adjuster adjustment, leaf spring spacers, shock absorbers, and aero dynamic shields if present.** You can either repeat everything or inform the inspector that the components on the right side are the same as the left side, with only a few differences on the tractor. If the inspector allows you to move on, proceed to step 10. However, if not, you will need to repeat everything on chapters 7 and 9 since they cover the same components, but on the opposite sides of the trailer.

Step 10

This is the final step in the walkthrough inspection before moving on into the in cab and air brakes inspection. Congratulations you one step closer to getting that class A license. So the finally components are as follow on the tractor passenger side.

The Exhaust- The exhaust system must be securely mounted with all clamps and bolts in place. The exhaust pipes must not be bent, cracked, or damaged.

The Heat Shield- The shield should be securely attached to a support bracket with all bolts in place, and should not have any damages.

Exhaust Supporting Rod- For tractors with a vertical exhaust, check that the exhaust components located behind the cab and connected to the exhaust bracket are not bent, cracked, or broken. There should be no signs of exhaust leaks or black smoke.

The DPF (Diesel Particulate Filter)- You can mention this component as it is connected with the exhaust system. These filters are responsible for cleaning out all the soot from the exhaust system, allowing clean air to exit the exhaust. Without going into detail, just mention that it has all the bolts and is not damaged in any way.

Walkthrough Conclusion

his marks the end of the outside inspection walkthrough. If nything was missed, it may be covered in my online course. Please el free to email me if you have any questions while preparing for ur exam. I hope that this walkthrough has provided you with a ear understanding of what needs to be said and how to say it in der to pass the exam. I also understand that some trucking hools may require more attention on this topic, so by studying this ok and taking my online course, you will have more time to focus driving during trucking school.

IN CAB INSPECTION

The inspection of the cab involves identifying the various small components both inside and outside the cab. It is a quick and easy test to clear before proceeding to the air brakes examination. As you enter the cab with the inspector, the first step is to ensure safety. Let them know that you will begin the examination by fastening your seat belt. Wearing seat belts is crucial as it demonstrates that you prioritize safety as a driver. Once both of you have fastened your seat belts, you can proceed with the cab inspection.

Steering Wheel-Make sure the steering wheel is securely fastened and has no more than one and a half inches of play. Test both the air and electric horn to demonstrate their functionality to the instructor.

Fire extinguisher- The fire extinguisher should be inspected to ensure that it is pressurized and fully charged, with the gauge indicating in the green range rather than the red. It's also important to check if it has been used before by looking for the presence of a yellow zip-tie on the pin. In addition, the reflective triangles and a box of spare fuses should be present inside the cab, as they are critical safety items that must not be overlooked.

Sun visor/ Windshield- The windshield should be inspected to ensure it is free of cracks and any unauthorized stickers. Additionally, verify that the sun visors

re securely mounted and that the sun visor clips are holding them
n place.

he Cab Top- Everything is sealed and properly and no cuts or torn
arts in the cab. The weathers strips on the door are secure and
verything is working properly.

Seat Belts / Buckles-The seat belts must be
roperly secured and in good condition without
ny cuts, rips or frays. Also, ensure that all the
ardware is present and securely mounted.

**Dashboard-The dashboard must be
hecked for secure mounting without any
gns of damage such as bending, cracking, or
reaking, and with all bolts intact. Additionally,
nsure that the A/C vents are functioning
roperly and not broken, allowing for easy air
ow. It's also important to check that the
gistration and insurance documents are present in the
assenger compartment.**

Dashboard Gauges-Ensure that the
auges for the air conditioning and
uspension are functioning properly. Verify

that the window
gauges on the doors
are also working
properly. Check that
the fan gauges are in
good working order and functioning as
expected. Lastly, verify that the wiper and
washer gauges are working properly.

The Red Trailer Emergency/ Yellow Parking Brake- Both of the
ush buttons function correctly and there are no audible indications

of leaks from these release buttons. They are functioning correctly and are easily readable.

Seats- The seats are working properly and go up and down and adjust as needed. The mirrors are mounted and secure along with the convex mirror. If they need to be adjusted they can be adjusted before beginning the drive test.

Pedals/Floorboards-The floorboards are intact with no cuts, rips, or tears. The pedals are secure and also free from any cuts, rips, or tears.

The Shifter-The shifter must be in the neutral position and working properly, and it should be securely attached without any signs of cracks or damage. The shifter boot must also be securely mounted on the floorboard to prevent any gases from entering the cab.

Instrumental Cluster- After verifying that all small components inside and outside of the cab are properly secured, proceed to check the gauges. The speedometer should work properly

and the needle should cycle when the key is turned. The tachometer and primary and secondary gauges should also cycle when the key is turned on, indicating the psi of the air tanks which

should be at 120psi-140psi. The oil gauge will show between 40 to 50, and the temperature gauge should also be in working order. Ensure that all the gauges are working properly, and the needles for every gauge have cycled. Once you have completed this part of the in-cab inspection, you may proceed with the air brake test.

AIR BRAKE TEST

The air brakes test is the third and final test, following the walkthrough and in-cab inspection. This 7-step test must be performed in the order listed below: applied leakage test, low air warning device, spring brake test, check rate of air brake build-up, static leak test, testing parking brake, and test service brake. The first step is the applied leakage test.

To start, fasten your seat belt and inform the instructor that you will turn on the engine and run it until you reach the governor cut-out range of 120-140 psi. Make sure to inform them that the primary and secondary gauges are both at 130 psi as a precaution. Next, release both the yellow parking brake and red emergency brake, turn off the engine, and cycle the key to the "on" position without starting the truck. Allow the gauges to stabilize and inform the inspector that you are beginning the applied leakage test.

Hold down the brake pedal for one minute and count in your head while watching the gauges to ensure they do not drop more than 3 psi. The tractor-trailer cannot lose more than 3 psi once the brake pedal is pressed and the gauges have stabilized. After one minute, inform the inspector whether or not the truck lost more than 3 psi. If the truck lost more than 3 psi, it must be repaired before retesting. If the truck did not lose more than 3 psi, inform the inspector that the applied air brake test is complete and move on to the next test

Low Air Warning Device-After completing the Applied Leakage Test, keep the key in the "on" position for the next test. Begin by pressing the foot brake several times to fan off the air pressure until the low air warning device activates. This device will activate

with a buzzer, light, and flag, and it should come on before the air pressure drops below 55psi. You must inform the inspector that the light came on before the pressure dropped below 55psi. If the light comes on any lower, it may indicate a problem in the air brake system. Once the light comes on, stop fanning the brake pedal and inform the inspector when it was activated and at what psi. This will conclude the Low Air Warning Device Test.

Spring Brake Test- To conduct the spring brake test, ensure that the tractor parking brake and protection valve (red button) are released. Next, fan the brake pedal until the pressure drops to between 20-45psi, at which point the tractor parking brake button and protection valve should pop out. Once this occurs, inform the inspector and let them know the pressure at which the brakes activated. This will conclude the spring brake test.

Check The Rate Of Air Pressure Buildup-To conduct this test, ensure that the engine is running at a normal idle speed, which is between 600-900 rpms. Observe the gauges as they build up and note that between 85psi to 100psi, the build-up should occur within 45 seconds. Notify the inspector about the build-up time between 85psi-100psi and ensure that it does not exceed 45 seconds. Also, inform the inspector when the governor cuts out, indicating that the air tanks are at full charge.

Static Leak Test- Once the air tanks are fully charged, turn off the engine and release the brakes to let the system settle. Then, observe the needle gauge for 1 minute without pressing the brake pedal. The truck and trailer should not lose more than 3 psi during this time. Inform the inspector if the gauges do not drop more than 3 psi for the minute. This test does not involve pressing the brake pedal and is only for observing the gauge. Once completed, inform the inspector that the test is done and move on to the next one.

Test Parking Brake-To test the parking brake, first ensure that your seatbelt is fastened and set the parking brake. Then gently pull against it in a lower gear while driving to check if it holds. After that, put the gear back in the neutral position and inform the inspector that the parking brake worked properly and prevented the vehicle from moving forward. This will complete the parking brake test.

Test Service Brakes- After allowing normal air pressure to build up and releasing the parking brake, slowly move the tractor forward bout 5 feet at a speed of around 5mph. Then firmly apply the rakes using the brake pedal. Let the inspector know that the ehicle did not pull to the left or right when the brakes were applied. ulling to either side could indicate a potential issue with the brakes, uch as uneven wear. Once you have completed the service brake est and all 7 steps of the air brake system test, inform the inspector at that you will be turning off the engine. Turn off the engine and allow em to finish their paperwork and testing results.

IN CONCLUSION

conclusion, I want to express my gratitude for taking the time to ad my book and study guide. I hope that it provides you with elpful insights as you pursue your CDL. While I understand that my uide is just a small part of the process, I believe it can be a valuable source for anyone seeking to obtain their CDL. One of the reasons hy I created this guide is to make the process more accessible for ose who may not have the means to attend expensive trucking chools. Education is an essential part of this process, and I believe at together, we can achieve our CDL goals.It is important to member that safety is the top priority both on the road and during e exam. As CDL drivers, we have a significant responsibility to nsure the safety of all families on the road. I wish you the best of ck, and I am confident that with practice and repetition in naming nd describing the components during the walk-through and in-cab spection, you will pass your exam. I look forward to seeing you all ut there on the road.

ank you once again for reading this book. I hope it assists u in obtaining your Class A or B license. I am sharing my xperience from the field to provide as much help as ossible, and I trust this information will be as valuable to u as it has been for me. I am excited to meet those who oose to take my online class and to see you out there on e road again. Best of luck to all of you!

Made in the USA
Las Vegas, NV
01 March 2024

86593113R00024